SOMEBODY'S DAUGHTER

JASMINE GAMES

THE **BLACK SPRING**
PRESS GROUP

First published in 2024
An Eyewear Publishing book, The Black Spring Press Group
Maida Vale, London W9,
United Kingdom

Typeset with graphic design by Edwin Smet
Author photograph Jazmyn Chipman

ISBN 978-1-915406-47-7

Printed in UK

*Editor's note: the author has requested that American spelling and
grammar be used in this work.*

BLACKSPRINGPRESSGROUP.COM

To my sisters and my sistas
Black women who were too grown yet still growing

CONTENTS

DOUBLE DUTCH

I learned the ropes as a child.
Sitting between my mother legs,
the back of my neck on pelvic bone.
This is where I first learned that
to be a Black woman is to persevere through pain.

She would tell me
this is the hair I got,
and that I have to stop
being so tender-headed.

There are things my mom could not get into my thick skull
or braid tight into this scalp,
and there are some things my mom could make me know
like the pop of a bobo against my head
wrapping around the roots of my twist telling me
"Black looks good on you,"
and the clip at the end hollas
"Remember that."

Sometimes deciding who I am is hard
when the net on the veil is too murky.
I hoped someone could see through it
like mama really could make glass.

The veil on Black was pulled
off a long time ago,
and replaced with a satin bonnet.
This makes it easier to sleep at night
and keeps this hair from falling out.

To be Black
and to be woman
is merely a game of Double Dutch.
I am still learning how to skip the ropes.

A DISAPPEARING ACT

Drew was
the most important first
not because he was my first crush,
but because he was my first rejection.
His reason being:
I was black.
He was not.

In the first grade I discovered

                                Blackness.

Since that moment
I tried for so long to make myself similar.
Remember the old days.
A little Black girl
too eager to burn her scalp for the image.
The sound of
tender-headed cries,
the smell of
hot combs,
and the pop of
bobos
always accompanied
a voice proclaiming my hair was
too thick.
That girl wondered if she
could hang herself with
Carly's hair on the jungle gym.
She could never be like them.

I was not white,
but could blush myself pink
after the next one said
I'd be beautiful with my hair laid down.

My mind
slowing waxing,
I thought my skin
would marble over.

Alabaster treachery:
I was fitting in
by forgetting me.

I was
speaking properly
in the name of porcelain.
I could see my reflection
in his pale white skin.

By fifteen—
proud to be
spread under a boy
who swears he only likes
white girls.

POLYCYSTIC OVARIAN SYNDROME

I free-falled into puberty. My fifth-grade body unfolded and bled like I was gutted. Now gutless I go to school, and a boy tells me: if he must shave his mustache, then so should I. I do not tell him that the testosterone in my body makes me more of a man than he will ever be, but instead see red, and I wonder if everyone sees. I pluck chest hair, and scrape at my chin. My skin is not as comfortable as yours is. I carry this burden, gaining ten pounds every year. I find myself ashamed of the inevitable blood stain. Ashamed of the bald spots, and how my toe hairs could replace them. I look in the mirror and know that I will never resemble a pear or a coke bottle, or my skinny sisters, instead I am an apple. It does not keep the doctor away. The ghost of my womanhood drowns in this yearlong flood, and I wish that I can go with her. I drift away in this sea of red and begin to wonder if who I am is really me or the fault in my genes. I begin to self-diagnose. A cyst on my ovary busts, and I pee on a stick to humor myself. I cry—I cry more than I bleed. I question my faith, and I ask why me. I am tired, but I cannot sleep. I confront everyone. I get mad at the sun for rising, the standard I have to live by, you for being happy, and me for breathing. I try to be ladylike. I try to be pretty. I take a pill for the body and not for the mind. I refuse to try therapy. What else might come from this curse? You hold me, but my body never could process anything sweet. I am womaning, in defeat.

VASELINE ON MY LIPS

Make it look like lip gloss
Back in high school
Stuffed my bra with another bra
Titties wasn't big yet
Didn't have hips yet
Mama telling me my life is ruined
If I have kids yet
I leave the house covered up
And change when I get to school

DON'T BRING HOME

Nothing less than an A
Don't wander past our yard
Don't bring home no friends
They ain't your friends
Anyway.

Cover your chest up.
Why you advertising what's
Not for sale?
No skinny jeans.
No skirts above your knees.
You ain't easy, you ain't loose.

Got something to say?
Knock out your screws.
When we get in here?
You better fix your face.
Go say hi!
Don't nobody care about your day.

Listen, I do this
Because I love you.
Go get the belt.
Now pull your pants down.
But not for no boy.

Don't fall for no trick
You ain't no treat
Stuck in no little boy's teeth
And if you come home pregnant
Ima send you to your granny's,
And I told you how she beat.
Me, I had you young,

And I'll be damned before you
Make the same mistake.

Worry about them books.
Don't bring home no bad grades,
And you better not be lying.
A liar, a thief makes,
A thief, makes a murderer,
And I'll let you sit in that jail.
Act like I never heard of ya'.

Talking back to me?
A slap to my face.
Ain't no child of mine
Gonna talk to me that way.
I brought you into this world.
I'll take you out of it.
You know what they could've did to you?
And you acting like you proud of it?

I brought you into this world,
And they can take you out of it.
Not guilty, walk free
Faces smug, cause they proud of it.
Auction the gun they shot you with
Probably say you were a thug and a slut

Your innocence won't be the talk of it.
So, act like you got some home training.
Ain't always gonna be here
To protect my baby.

After school,
Come straight home
And don't bring nothing
Less than an A.

GOOD HAIR

The last time
I was told that my potential could not be reached,
because my hair was not straight,
I should have said:

This is the last time my own puts me on the bottom shelf.
Coffee complected beings can be as nasty as coffee itself.
Nor will some of us come to terms with the natural hair that we bare,
because some of us can't see past the glare of lustrous locks.

My hair lacks luster, but it is illustrious.
Thick to deflect the subjectivity people put me under.
Black and brown as the richest soil in a garden.
Standing high, aware of who is beneath it.
Strands intertwining, not falling into submission.

It took fifteen years for me
to know my mane is not a nest.
And I wonder
how many years it will take
for the next Black girl to love herself.
For the next Black strand
to not feel out of place.

For the next Black girl:
Realize
that a Black girl's hair is a statement itself,
so powerful it should not be touched.
that our confidence is up like an afro,
and will remain as strong as naps after a long day.

VIEWS FROM WASH DAY

Mother broke my neck over the kitchen sink.
"Nappy" is the hair that comes from a Black scalp.
Words were the fresh cut, shape up, silver glint
that cut at kinky twists. My kitchen now on all sides of me.

Hair that comes from a Black scalp is "nappy"
and sad was I who came to know this.
In the kitchen, mother cut what was kinky—
as if words did not do enough taking.

Sad was I to believe
desirable I'd be if my hair were straighter,
then let words take my crown and spirit.
The pain of the neck is minute beside the mental effects.

Desirable, a Black being,
that grew their hair with their own hands,
and healed their mind through their mane.
Washes their hair in the kitchen sink, neck full of kinks.

Love can grow in the right hands
words, a silver glint, sharp no more.
A kitchen sink full of "nappy."
A child that is not broken.

KEEP IT CUTE

I haven't thought about killing myself in a long time
and I think it scares me. How strange this feels.
Like contentment wasn't made for this body.
Keep this body busy. Always have a job.
Always somewhere to be. Someone to talk to.
What would I think of me,
if I thought for myself?

To this day,
I cannot live down my awkward stage.
Puberty hit me like a train; little white debris sprinkled
on my face, scalp tight with braids that came a loose
and braces tracked my teeth.

My mom used to tell me I was beautiful every day.
Her words like cup coasters used on scratched wood.
I could stare at a wall, and it would become a picture show,
illuminating an alternative to being in this body.
Stare for hours
my mom crying from the state of me.

One day pretty did come.
Could make the world my fool.
Yet at my grown age
shed tears for young me.

At least I was cute.
Couldn't tell me nothing.
Pain: I had bookoo.

But a glow up isn't all that
if your spirit don't glow too.
I learned that the hard way.
I don't want that for you.

DUPLEX FOR MY MOTHERS

My mama came out when I was young.
Indeed, two mothers are better than one.

Yes, I said: two mothers are better than one,
And Morgan gave me a second birth.

When you are born for the second time,
You leave the womb clean and forgiven.

Do not forget to cleanse with forgiveness;
Rebirth can be an ugly, messy thing,

But mamas don't raise ugly, messy things.
They let things soak until they are ready.

You know you are ready after soaking
When your fingertips begin to prune,

And mama got up when her fingers creased.
My mother came out when I was young.

SPOONFUL'S

I.
To be a mother is to be water
constantly transforming
into different versions of yourself while
maintaining who you are knowing that
you will have to be an ocean on days where
you are just enough to be a puddle.

II.
I am afraid one day I will drown
in the matter that you are,
seeing if I can hold my breath
longer than you can hold yours.
I will gargle on the memories
we never created.
I will regret not ever
learning how to
                    swim
in the resentment
that is now
cemented to me,
pulling me into
the darkest depths
of confrontation.

III.
Do not call yourself
a mother,
but instead, a hurricane,
displacing everyone
close to you,

only to cycle
back into
your habits.

IV.
You are not the ocean
just the oil spill,
and I cannot breathe in
this water torture cell.

MUSTARD SEED

This is not the first time
she has faltered through prayer.

She prays about as many times
as she actually believes she
is praying to a God that is there:
not much.

She speaks into the air hoping
that her words will be like Holy Ghost,
and someone will want to catch them.

This prayer is half a sob,
halted in the back of a throat
at the height of a gospel song.
This prayer is for all the times
she saw how faith changed a life.
It is for all the times she thought
she never could be saved.
This prayer is lifting up praise
with half-open palms and heavy arms,
still uncertain.

"Look at your neighbor,"
but never really know them.
She does every Sunday.

Her mom reminds her
that in this home
they will praise the Lord.
No one talks about exactly
how, or reassures any doubts.

Do not question the Lord
only question yourself.
"What you got to be sad
for when God put a roof
over your head?"
This prayer is
for her mind
that never seemed to be
touched by him.

For the nights she has spoke
to the ceiling,
but never really felt like
she was praying.

For all of her broken
spilt across the
kitchen tile,
family a witness
to her snap.

For her being on her knees,
yet again,
thinking she can find The Father
in a taking man.

She will not
say Amen
at the end of this prayer,
instead she will feel foolish—
put herself together,
lift herself from the ground,
and not know
who will save her.

A WOMAN LIKE MS. BRENDA

Ms. Brenda was the first
transwoman I truly knew.
Met her at church,
we had a mutual respect for the church
aisle as a runway.
She complimented my church suit.
Plaid with gold stitching
I wore it once a month.
I complimented her hair,
wavy and a bit red.

She told me her story
of how she is a woman
despite being considered the manliest of men
and she taught me something but
I didn't know then.
Women are strong too.
She still worked at a construction site,
and I, so young and bright
loved Ms. Brenda.
One of my first friends,
we shared birthdays
only saw each other on Sundays.

I hoped I could be a woman like her.
Not taking no shit from a group of men.
I was in elementary school,
but I could understand.
Brenda was a woman because she said so,
and I thought I'd be like her.
Unfortunately, I'd just never be that tall,

but in some ways,
I could take up space like her.
Let you be happy I did.

I haven't seen Ms. Brenda since I was a kid,
but she stays on my mind.
She will always be missed.
Wherever she is,
I wish her love and happiness.

She didn't know it,
but she was my only friend.
My parents divorced.
Another woman, with her,
my mom moved in.
That house we lived in—
never saw again.
For a little, sent letters
but eventually, ain't had no friends.
Bullied at the new school
because I was not in.

But Ms. Brenda,
Beautiful Brenda:
was my Sunday resonance.

GREATER CITY, TEXAS

unused locks on doors and the kids running through them
mamas who yell about their good air and a glass of water
Old Faithful and Black Beauty slinging slapping butts red
big belts that whooped generations into shape no rod spared

bologna and white bread Hostess treats and frosted flakes
sugar in spaghetti and in rice and in grits *and* in kool-aid
life expectancy low heartache and attack in the same home

Saturday morning sung awake Etta James and Marvin Gaye
bleach and lavender dusting mopping sweeping washing
crying complaining muttering under breath sneaking sleep
the drag of incense perhaps a wax candle the smell of clean

Sunday mornings ruffles on white socks puffy pink dresses
soft lace between two fingers smile for the camera repeat
vacation bible school Easter Sunday bible camp John 3:16

shoes to grow into friends to grow out of babies grow in
the people stay forever or never come back again until then
some finish school some still taking classes at community
ignoring each other at the grocery store pushing baskets

humble but never modest parents who made it out the ward
kids who die for a hood they never lived in gang banging
suburban thugs gunshots neighborhood tragedy no not him

valedictorians scholars and gifted children honors and sad
dean's list daddy issues dick slangin' and political debates
new job new friends no parents no hometown new rules
excellence advocacy organizing economy C's get degrees

unfamiliar people city ain't the same highway with 8 lanes
remember the trees smell fast food remember field fed up
could've been anyone and it didn't take you. How great.

THINGS FALL APART

I.
We grew up together,
walking to school
when we missed the bus.
Catching crawfish in the ditch,
we loved sixth grade science club.
I had a crush on him because
he liked things it wasn't cool
for Black kids to like yet.
Though he wanted my best friend.
I chose his friendship instead.

When we got to high school
he was not a science club kid.
He was football player fine.
Hazel eyes and hot temper.
Friend to all but will still
Whoop yo ass in the cafeteria.
Though he would say hello
to his long-lost nerd friends
passing in the hallway briefly.

And we were not friends always,
but close we were walking home
close we were spending summers
playing football in the pool.
Close we were seeing each other
for the first time in a long time
at our younger siblings'
high school graduation.
I ain't even know he had kids.
That was the last time I saw him.

Title after *Things Fall Apart* by Chinua Achebe and 'The Second Coming' by Yeats

The headline said,
"Man found shot to death in driver's seat of car"
Someone in the comments said,
*"This is why I am always alert
and watching out everywhere.
Like I am a very paranoid person.
I don't even sit with my back to people
and if I am then I'm always
turning around to see who is around me."*

II.
I was dating his son.
I never got to meet him.
He did his work in Sunnyside
not the type to bring that life
back home to his children.
He did what he had to do
like many people got to do.

I was told he went to college
fathered a few children.
With his support
many people had a better living.
And he meant the world to his son,
who lost his mother young.
They say he looks just like his father,
but I only ever saw the pictures.

I remember being jealous
that my boyfriend got
lunch money every day,
an allowance to spend.
I always wanted a parent
who allowed for that independence.
I remember wiping his tears

in the passing period.
The bell rang minutes before.
He just stood there, not moving,
staring in my eyes with his own sunken ones.
I said nothing, but rubbed my thumb across his face,
catching teardrops before they lost their shape.

The headlines said,
"Drug Dealer Shot in South Houston"
"Thug Fallen in Shootout"
Someone in the comments said,
"Three down and about 25,000
left to go in Harris County.
Now if they would just cooperate
and kill each other we'll be doin'
a lot better crime wise!"

BLACK THEATRES

the collective breath
hell naws and don't do its
full plates in the imax
smacking on fingers
yelling at the same time
hell naw and don't do it
it ain't just the movie
that makes the show
all the people in a row
making it a night you
wish to remember
like reading the review
while watching the movie
you with your friends
and y'all getting to it
looking fine for the
moment when the lights
come up in the theatre
cussin out the one viewer
who didn't know better
than to shush someone
during the viewing
and you won't recall
that one movie
but you'll remember
the people
at that one theatre
on that one street
you got to
go there
again.

NEARLY NATURAL

In the living room of what once was my mother and father's home,
Plants with everlasting posture are positioned.
Plastic, nearly nature mistaken for the leaves of a real plant,
Dust serving as pollen to the potted decor disappears:
Cleanliness is close to Godliness.
                              This is how I have learned to present myself

Every December, the artificial fir
Is taken from the storage,
And propped up in the fore room.
This way, the Christmas spirit
Is not cast out without intention.
There are funeral flowers that
Are not pressed into bibles
                                        Because failure of preservation
Will not be the last petal plucked in mourning.

The upkeep of a faux plant is tedious, unexpectedly.
Dust can be swept away but will timely return.
I have polished my personality,
Pinned the corners of my mouth in a smile,
Purchased clothes to make myself presentable,
Yet this facade leaves me with no life, and
                              Makes me a disservice to my existence.

WINTER FUNERAL

It snowed in Texas
the day I left for Wisconsin,
and there I found no snow.
Still, my eyes icy at the sight of it.

Joe, I sat in the bed you
passed away in,
and I wondered if you knew
that the final night
would be your last.

Did you take a last look
at the ageing
Green Bay Packers memorabilia
and know your season was over?

Frozen in place,
"Never Would Have Made It"
played in my head
and my body shivered from sobbing.
Unfamiliar to a Wisconsin winter,
I thought that one day we'd
chill here together.

Some days,
I am falling apart
all at once
like an avalanche.
My heart burns like
hot water over
frost bitten hands.

I found that there
is not a coat big enough
for a winter storm.
I can shovel the snow,
but tiny snowflakes will return
to trap me where I stand.

It snowed in Wisconsin
the day of your funeral,
and I have not stopped
feeling cold since.

TO POPPA JOE FROM YOUR CHILDREN

After "To Aunt Rose" by Allen Ginsberg

Poppa Joe—now—might we see you
with your joyous face and the balls on your cheeks
and pain of your heart—and a long black belt
that whipped at Joie, Mandy, and Jasmine
as we ran past the football game
in the crowded living room
there was no other route to take
and how we wish to be back there with you.
Your heavy footsteps would lead to the
recliner chair no matter what room it was
or would make a running jump to squeeze the
life out of us on that one single queen size bed.

—Big Joe
you stood so tall
(and for most years so wide)
—scared our friends so bad,
they wouldn't even speak
when you answered the door.
You scared a whole football team
over Marwan's broken finger.
The strongest man we knew
would never sugarcoat his words
could fix anything
(he built his own computer from scratch)
loved all his kids—and his grandkids
loved Jhanay even when she was a teenager
going through her angsty stage.
At a time where he could have shied away,
he loved harder.
Tough love was always so tough,

but ever so genuine.
Took all Rhawnie's friends in,
treated them as his kids (and who would tell him differently)
was the only person at Rhawnie's birthday party,
Uncle Jason and him.

Joe
the packers will go all the way
the packers will win a super bowl
you will cheer from your grave
you will rejoice in heaven.

Though we see you driving still, a Cadillac on Coit Rd.
bumping rap, old and new
limping a little with a smooth smile,
one arm out the window
in what must have been the
best outfit you owned: all blue.
Mandy waited on you—see you arriving
with that bike of hers.
Jhanay waited on you—see you arriving
with the snickers bar for every babies' arrival
(even when you weren't there yourself).

Dance Dance Revolution, pawnshops, Madden,
movies, Big Mama's Chicken
all the places in Milwaukee we may have never been to
they all suddenly feel like home.
Mandy and Jasmine will graduate just as you asked of them,
they will imagine holding your hand across the stage,
just as you would hold theirs in church
a single tear down your face.
We shed the tears now.

Last time we all were together
was at Joie's graduation.
Your brown skin glowing
yet again in that all blue outfit.
Quick-witted comebacks,
funnier than ever.
We will remember you happy,
but it sure was too soon.

BIG AND BLACK

Joe's favorite entertainers
were big and Black
sitting in front of an old big screen tv,
he seen me entranced by the light animation
bumping to "Juicy."

He'd say
Biggie was better than Tupac.
Was he biased? Perhaps.
See, him and Biggie:
both big and Black
boisterous brothas.

After the divorce, my dad
didn't listen to rap music for months,
gospel music shook the house
until Joe had to shake us.
Marvin Gaye plays
everyone lifts their hands to praise.
"Never Would Have Made It"
haunts me to this day
the way my dad sang it on the phone
a few hours before he couldn't hold on
a few months before Joe wasn't looking big,
more grey than Black.
a few times before his heart attack.

My dad did not die big,
yet in my memory he is still four hundred pounds,
scaring my friends who come to the door to play,
making the Cadillac ride low,

and slowing the line up three stories to that
one-bedroom apartment.

No, he is not the thin hand I helped down the curb.
He was a big, Black, boisterous brother.
Leaning back in his computer chair,
sipping a forty-four,
watching Rob Dyrdek's Fantasy Factory.

Rest in peace Big Black, who died
a year before Joe, went out the same way.
Hearts ain't built to support all that weight,
but my dad loved to see that man's joy.
Call it an escape.

"Aston Martin Music": the ringtone.
We were eating off my sister's stamps
but you couldn't tell that man he wasn't luxurious.
He too,
breezed down the freeway,
just him and his babies
in his ride.*
It wasn't no
Aston Martin,
but you couldn't say shit
about his
Cadillac,
his kids,
his big,
and Black.

* After "Aston Martin Music" by Rick Ross

SONNET FOR SOMEBODY'S DAUGHTER

May you be protected and held by love,
so when your heart breaks, you will not undo.
May you never want for nothing, enough
of who can't provide—not checkin' for you.

You be everything you ever needed.
I realize it is not easy alone.
In life, fathers are our first male allies,
and some men aren't able for those seeded.

For thyself, may you learn how to forgive.
I pray you see you and feel home within
feel peace, feel whole, rooted and born again.
What you want in this life, you will achieve.

Whatever is truly for you, it will be.
Love, I hope you know you were made complete.

I DON'T THINK

We can choose who we love

Or else maybe I would've loved
Many before
And maybe I told myself I could
Love someone besides you

But I don't think
We can choose who we love
And this is why I still love
Those who've hurt me
Those I don't agree with
Those I hope will one day come around

See we can't choose who we love
But honey
If we could
I'd still choose
you.

ROMANTIC COMEDY

in my imagination I am on the way
and you are waiting for me at the arrival gates
and we meet again for the first time
because every time is different.

under one small umbrella,
we walk in the rain for ice cream.
in one small apartment,
we dress up and run late
order the meat lovers plate.
make it to the subway.
talk about the world,
participate in debates.
we agree to disagree.

we go dance. too many, I drink.
I am laid in your lap, asleep in the cab,
and you hate it, but you are there for me.
we cuddle before we separate.
you are in my dreams even laying next to me.

we imagine the big day.
foresee our future.
where will we wed?
we find middle ground
though we are not on the same land.

I long to hold your hand.
I forget how your skin feels
but I know it is where I belong.
I fell for you without knowing who you were.

often, I am afraid the distance will create dissonance.
but I choose to believe the best things arrive on delay.

but every time I must leave:
the worst part about seeing you
is having to go away.

in my imagination I board the plane
you try not to, but you love the chase
you run down the aisle before I leave
and like a perfect romantic comedy
crazily, you say—marry me.

BLACK LOVE MATTERS

Everything I love about you
I love about myself.
Our noses wide and our
eyes almost black
they are so brown.
Our strands of hair love
one another so much
they are hard to pull apart.

You know,
I run my hands
through your afro.
It is soft like
a dandelion,
but strong enough
to never be uprooted.

My wish is to always
be able to do
this here with
you.

Our skin could never be
called dirty;
when we press together
all that is left between us
is something *inexplicable*—
so *revolutionary*—
and *pure*.
We thirst for each other's
                Black
was always made a monster,
but we know Black
absorbs so much light.
And *we, are fulgent*.

PORTRAITURE FOR HEAVY HANDS

The only love I knew,
could turn Black skin blue.
Hold her hand
to hold her down.
Your lovely sentiments,
but cemetery wishes

The only love I knew,
took my mother
and sisters too.

I know men
to have two faces,
neither ever expressing
guilt.

I know wide white smiles,
that have fangs at night.
Taking and taking,
until she feels she has nothing left.
                Not even herself.

I know women
to be canvases,
made striking
then hung up
            for show.

I know I am
not an exception
to this art form.
The women I know
have been made more
colors than their skin tone.
But I cannot be

your muse.

I USED TO LOVE SLEEPOVERS

as a kid until you peed in your sleep and now you friend knows
you still piss the bed when embarrassed I wish I was dead
and my mama said don't laugh at me like you ain't never peed your pants
before it's like laughing at yourself to laugh at your friend in the same predicament
you've found yourself in and what do sleepovers look like now that nobody pees

do you know sometimes I can barely sleep?

I shake at night.

Sometimes I scream.

I fist fight fitted sheets there's someone sitting on me I feel it when I wake

Would you laugh at me?

to know there are scarier things
that happen in my sleep than releasing a stream
my mama said call her anytime of the night
she will stay up until I fall
how funny it is that I still seek my mama in the dark.
when I'm scared I want to die.
so it's just like old times and back in the day
we feared monsters under the bed
and now I'm scared of the monsters people become on top of them
the ones you never forget because they visit you in your sleep
and I bet all the while they don't lose any
and when we were kids, we held hands under the covers to know we were safe

Would you think I was weird if I wanted you to hold me as we lay?

LITTLE WATER CLEARS US OF THIS DEED

I hold my breath in my sleep
when I see you there.
Scrub my skin from your teeth
get you off of me.
When you're in my dreams,
I fear for me,
and if that is the love
then I hate this poem
for coming to me as I sleep.
I can't leave you even
in a place where I make my own.
Gotta get your love off of me.

Again, I say I don't want you.
Let me die on this belief.
Take a good thing
and let it die deep.
Everything good ain't for me.
My heart beat in my sleep
when I see you there.
You could've killed me.

If this is the love poem
I've been trying to write
then what is love?
Some cum-stained poetry
that comes in the night.
We fucked in the day.
Haunt me in a reverie.
And you haven't been here
and you're still at my place

clicking bones from the closet
letting the drag back in
sitting on my chest
waking me up

from a good thing.
Reminding me,
I don't deserve shit.
Making me think
maybe I ain't the one
for anybody.
Waking me up
on the wrong side,
whichever side that be.

In a life with the perfect one,
can't untie some string.
I had to cut you off,
please take your leave.

I held my breath in my sleep
trying to kill a good thing.
Don't know if I'm being told
to forgive you or forgive me,
but I cannot die this way.

I just can't give up
the real thing
to walk in my sleep.

SEND MY APOLOGIES TO MS. JACKSON

First of all,
I tried my best to love your son told him the last time will be the
last time he messed it up so many damn times and I still tried to
love him

Second of all,
I understand the plight of a black man but who will save me why
I'm steady trying to save him and to be honest I was really scared
of him you don't see what he do when he get mad I don't see him
anymore in the ring of his eyes I have no choice but to fear him but
even that didn't make me leave the first time

On his mama,
You know he done lied on you so much it's a miracle you still here
and don't get me started on his granny's grave may her soul rest in
peace despite her grandson's antics

Anyways,
Truly he was my best friend knew me better than any man knew
my blessings knew my sins and I fucked with him so bad people
said I ain't have no sense but here I am and I know people think I
romanticized him and all but they don't see every part of your son
like we do you and I both know he could be better because we've
seen it but ma'am we both know your son wouldn't love me
through my bad sides like I've loved that man through his and boy
were they bad bad

And the funny thing is,
I left because he was tryna slide on one of his best friend's girl got
damn how many times did he cheat before I caught him slippin

And the sad thing is,
When I saw you fawning over some man that was not the one you
wed I knew infidelity was inherited passed down and he would
never live up to any lover I dreamed of him being

Believe you me,
I wanted to love your son even if it killed me and I know you
wanted me to love him anyways even after all you knew he done
but remember that night you looked me in my eyes and said I got
to love myself I had to shake your son for my health would've
gave that man so many beautiful little girls but I guess the world
got enough Ms. Jacksons

RECOLLECT YOURSELF

I forgot I was a morning person I forgot what
the sun looks like when it is rising

the sun forgot me it touches me through my
windowsill, and it can't quite remember my

name is Jasmine a foolish thing to prescribe
to your love as if

the sun was not enough I stand right
underneath it and

absorb nothing of substance comes from a
person who forgot what they

looked like in good lighting forgot what they
sound like without

a lead singer who forgets the feeling of their
own floor

beneath their bare feet nothing built on
quicksand ever stood

still can you not tell I have been sinking or
could you not hear me

because I forgot I had a voice too I forgot I
was a morning person

and I can only remember how the sun looks
when it is sinking

I forgot I could wake up at seven AM like it
was nothing but I can recall

that now that it's the fourth day in a row and
it's seven AM and I am clawing at my
bedsheets and I am

                        crying

and

      I cannot

recall

        what   for

BLACK GIRL'S DECREE

I thought my skin was poppin'
before hashtags made it popular.
I loved my hair
before YouTube told me how to copy em'.
My black was beautiful
before you exclaimed.

Put some respect on my name.
Don't mistake the surname,
I do not play no games.
Try me and get played,
but bitch this ain't spades.
Used to call me nappy headed
now you wanna know my ways.

Try to wrap me up,
and get twist out.
You silk pressed?
Get popped in the mouth.

I'm on my cocky shit
because I love who I am.
I do this without trying.
They tried to kill me,
but I'm not dying.

No kids,
but call me mother.
Tried to kill me,
but I'm only tougher.

All the Black ladies before me
and the ones after
hope you know that
your life matters.
They talk all that shit,
but we still excel.
You can't shut me up.
Ima make it known.

Before you tell me about myself
better check your own.
I am my own trophy.
Fuck a shelf, where's my throne?

SLUTS GET THE BEST GRADES

Cuz we know how to get an A
Pop pussy on college ruled
Paper come in multiples
Personality on multitudes
Stay up all night
Bustin books open
To do good in school

Touching ourselves
In tutorials
Accomplishing goals
At the club
Checking canvas
Beating blackboard
Better get it in by 11:59
Stay up all night then we 69
All the while be way too fine

Professor know you a dime
Wake up an hour early to beat your face
Never know when you'll run into your soulmate
They hit you up for the test answers
Only give it up if they a dancer
Valedictorian how you number 1
These niggas be thirsty
They ready to love
At the college party
Stalking your ass
But you leave a little early
Cause in the morning you got class

They hating saying we won't make it
Say don't dress like that
How you gonna get hired
With your titties out
Ass fat in them office pants
Ring in your nose
Tattoo on your breast
And still acing every test
Bad bitch getting interviewed
Boss like you she into you

I told you sluts get the best grades
You know what to do if you want an A

DEAR BLACK ACTRESS,

"Thank you for auditioning for"—

"We regret to inform you that"—

"You weren't quite what we were
looking for"—

Rejection is the cause of the trapdoor accident that crippled your self-worth.
Your talent is exceptional, but your look won't fit the
        Alabaster vision.
They will give the role to that same girl:
She she she blonde she she button nosed she blue eyed.
She's rarely ever Black, never you
And white pedestal placing excused as creativity
Is the trend that has nine lives.
Whitewash is the new Black.
Still, they will admire your skill
That's never worth anything
More than supporting roles.
Remember:
There are no small parts, just small actors.
I mean—
There are plenty of small parts reserved for minority actors.

Dammit Black Actress,
You should have known better.
You sat in a green room and felt blue
As they laughed
Saying "the only way to play the Black character is to be ghetto."
When you tell them how their jaws snap,
Their crocodile tears won't be
As convincing as the sound of their cackles.

All the world's a stage,
And Black Actress you cannot take direction from the same
          white girl
Without feeling like your people oppressed
Without feeling the uproar in your throat squeezed by the
Noose in hers.

You are an outlier:
Insignificant in this Black Box.
Fade into those walls,
Your skin so dark they will not notice
Or will say they didn't:
"I never would have thought you would be this good."
Prejudice crawls from their mouths and
Makes home in your self-esteem.
You will not be afforded the privilege of
Consideration before the audition.

So instead, Black Actress,
Act as if this is the work of an activist
And your presence is radical.
Your presence is radical
In a world where Hattie McDaniel was not offered
A Seat at the Table.
You will not get a Viola Davis moment,
Remaining complacent,
Playing nice to your opponents.
The white woman,
Frolicking *in green fields and lovely flowers,*
Has arms only half-stretched out like
Just enough effort to call herself an ally,
Knowing you deserve more
But sacrifices justice for stage time.
So you must take it from them.
Snatch all edges,

A Black woman's pastime,
Which is to say,
Scalp all of your victims.
Hang those golden tresses up on a wall
Like it is the only trophy you will ever need.

This is the civil rights movement
Behind a red curtain.
This is the Black child rebelling
Against the American upbringing.
This is a strong Rosa Park's
        No
That sounds more like
A terrible difficult thing to say
But a harder thing still to do.
        You, Black Actress,
Were made to play more than
Slave than single mom than victim.
You are thespian in the Black flesh.
You are not yet the actor center stage,
But you are the spotlight.

So speak up, Black Actress.
Your voice must
Ring like freedom.
Projecting your voice
Is second for the stage
First for self-preservation
For the Black woman.

And if they won't cast you then
Shonda Rhimes the hell out
Of the industry.
Colonize their bigotry
With so much Black girl magic,

Tituba will live again
And cast a spell
To split the tongues
That dared to raise
In malice against
A Black woman.

Black Actress,
You are the aftermath of
Years of disacknowledgment
And they aren't ready for your
Wake.

THE QUEEN MOTHER'S NECK

Must hurt.

To lift a head
That is not hers.
Lead by eyes she
Must trust to see.

Wondering when
The man will ever
Carry his own head.

Taking orders from
Those less qualified
Than her.

Must tense.

To be gaslit,
Told she really
Has all the power
But it's better if the
Man is the face of it.

Must long.

To be familiar
To the headless horseman
Searching for what
Was took from her.

WHITE NOISE

News of death,
told as often as bedtime stories,
but this will not help the sleep deprived.

We lie awake,
watching,
white men carry white chalk,
magic wands to draw the death
before the Black bodies will ever see it.

Say the magic words,
or say nothing at all,
because Black bodies
will fade into chalk lines
before they live to defend themselves.

Somewhere—
cops play hopscotch
with their kill count.
While Black bodies count how much time they have left.

You will not wake to survive nightmares like this.

How do you escape
the six feet of dirt
shoved down your throat?

A Black child knows the power
of living to eighteen.
A White man knows a spell
to make nineteen never.

And never,
will a Black body stand in the presence of forever.
They will meet the reaper,
prior to knowing God.

We continue to put hope in a magic hat of equality,
when nothing adorable comes from it.
Nooses vanish in plain sight.
A magic trick
called white privilege.

When you finally go to sleep,
and all that remains is white noise,
understand that you sleep on racism,
as it puts us to rest.

I CRIED FOR DAYS

guilt of the helpless
      Witness
Black men on pavement
breath billowing blastedly
and I, holding my own,
seeing this through a screen,
cannot stop crying
like it was someone I knew—
like it was my brother
lying in the street
stolen in broad daylight
by white men whose
freedom is already accounted for.
who can:
run down the street
play with toy guns
drive through stop signs
when endangered, call the police
watch tv in their living rooms
out of cars, sell CDs
resist arrest
walk free.

MY PEOPLE

Do not feel bad
for refusing to feel bad.
Not feeling,
in this country,
can save you from yourself.
It is numbness
that helps you heal.

My people,
do not feel bad
for the unsaved draft.
I know you are enraged
but speechless.
Voice hoarse from
saying the same damn thing
over and over and over
again.

My People,
the greatest sob
will take the breath from your lungs,
and you ain't done grieving yet.

So accept the break
your spirit is giving you,
but remember there will come
a time to clock back in.

My people,
they will not
do the work,
and in this country,
you must work to live.

FLETCHER MARTIN'S *DOWN FOR THE COUNT*

Down:
the gift for condition
boxing African Americans
smoky lived depression
count career
the cause:
racism in America
men in conflict
experiencing trauma
before his time
these men
not on a
level playing field.
Life.

UNFIT BLACK VICTIMS

If you say her name,
do not make it so
you must say it again.

Say it right by her,
whoever she is
or how she became her.

She who dies the same
as all Black victims do,
deserves the same rage
as Black men accrue.

There should be no reason
why that cop can go on vacation,
when she had a life before his taking.

Too many of us are guilty of
forgetting who they are.
When any Black person leaves us
by the hands of the oppressor,
we cannot continue to neglect them.

Think of all the names
we did not know to know,
and all the ways

                                        unfit Black victims
                              die
                  alone.

                    Without protest.
        Without demands.
                                    No hashtag or petition.
              No funds for conviction.

We stay quiet in this nation.
                              It's a shame.
            Whether an angel or a vixen,
                    no one should die in the system.

Ask yourself,
who is an ideal victim?
If you have an answer,
then it is as bad as I predicted.

FAST FOOD

I don't stir the pot
I serve the pot
season it a little
what America made
been on the stove too long
now no one wants to eat it.
you ignore the pot
while it sits and stews
does that
   sound fair

      to you

please, after you.
take a bite
    of

      your privilege

          too

sorry, if you don't like
the food
that nourishes you
but you cannot return to sender
so eat it up and eat it well
because a new cook is in

      the kitchen

NO NOTHIN'

i don't owe white people nothin'.
i don't owe them
my body,
my presence,
my intellect,
my insight,
a thank you,
a compliment,
gratitude,
admiration,
no nothin'.

i done went to they school.
got my education and got out.
i love my education, but i do not love those people.
i know they do not love me.
i know that when they do,
it is only to show out.

i do not owe them
my Black recommendation—
no alumni vindication.

i don't owe white people nothin',
no nothin'.
not a damn thing.
ima get what i need
to go where i need,
and then ima dip.

plain and simple.

MOTHER, DON'T WORRY

I will have a career.
Somebody will hire me.
I am not a people pleaser
not polite unconditionally
not holding water in my mouth
for those who seek to drown me
and not making a dollar for a company
who pinch pennies from the population.
Will not smile when my coworker pets my hair.
Will not laugh at the provoking Trump joke.
Will not work for those people.

I do not judge you for what you must do
to feed those you gave birth to,
but me, I will die broke before working
miserably at a job for a check that does
not check on me, sitting furious on a
lunch break I do not get paid for,
making eight dollars an hour
eight hours a day forty hours a week
holding in a fury that deforests follicles
from my scalp. It is not worth it.
I rather die broke than die compliant.

We do not have to work this way anymore.
What is professional? Codeswitching for
a coworker, acting like I am one of those
that don't talk like that. Wearing ill-fitting
clothes because my body is sexualized
senselessly. Putting in excessive labor
to prove a hard-working spirit to an

employer who will promote those
inferior to you. Saying yes because no
could mean termination.

How we give power to a damn table
of all places. The seat is not the finish
line. The table is crowded, and why should
we go to dinner with racists? Let us build
shelter for our people who can come as they
are and work as they want and get paid properly.
We have wealth in our community.
We do not work for free.
We work with freedom.

TO MY PROFESSOR

who said I wasn't a good writer,
well, I don't think
you make a good African American
(he was white as hell y'all
speaking on Black people like
he knew better than us Black people)
yet you get to teach this AA Lit course.
So I am going to continue to write.
And I would say one day you'll
teach my poetry to your students
but you was old as hell when you taught me
so you'll probably be dead by then

and that makes me happier than ever
because you don't deserve anything I've written.

COUNTER-MEMORY

I think of Black History. To be clear, I ain't referring to no Black History that is shared to us through white media and educational institutions, tellin' us what really had happened and how we should feel about it. I am talking about that Black History that I would have never known if my father's mother's mother had never told. Those who are and were old enough to remember. To live through it. To hear about it when they were a kid. The history that is buried, burned, and belittled. And, the history that was struck out of backs so much that mouths would not open and bodies could not remember how they once moved. Minds could not remember how we as people made thoughts in our heads that were not put there. History that told a culture that did not make it through slavery like some of the slaves who did, despite not knowing what they can't remember. And we are born with all this forgot. Just tryin' to know something the way we should remember. And not havin' the ability to recall while Black is to be lost. And some of us lose ourselves to be knowing.

BETTERING

look back to look forward
this is the life lived
and it is a beautiful thing
to have made it

despite the struggle
the bathroom breakdowns,
lukewarm bathwater
and suicidal thoughts,
letters to home and to loves,
bag packed to run away

those who survive more than pass
who have youth to waste away
did not spend it at the young age
dance in the place you stand
then dance again

because you thought you would not
make it this far and you did.
you thought the light would not shine
and it shimmered.
you thought you would never grow old,
and you are old enough
to know
life is a beautiful thing
and you lived long enough
to smell the flowers
and breathe deep
to take a walk
and come home
to look in the mirror

and look away
to go to sleep
and wake up
to know who you are
and love yourself

and it took a few years,
but no one can take it from you.
Life is a beautiful place.

WHAT MAKES YOU GROWN

Did it all on your own,
left the roof called home,
walked across the city to make it,
saw something most don't see.
Innocence expired and
childhood was over.
Isolation bred impatience.

You made a choice for yourself.
You pay your own bills.
You don't ask nobody for nothing.
You are working on yourself.
You are about that age now.
You did something you can
never come back from.

Childbirth came soon.
Aged by heartbreak.
Crisis hit as a young adult.
You left adolescence
and returned someone else.

Or maybe,
you know when you know,
but one thing is for sure:

You ain't grown until you grow.

CRAVING SOFTNESS

"I've done the strong black woman thing, but I'm craving softness"- Amanda Seales

I am not old enough to be this tired,
and I told myself I would not cry
when I wrote this.

Yet, here I am
with clenched fists and soft hands
runny nose on pretty skin,
trying to woman like this.

A lot of things bother me
that I pretend do not.
Like how people
would like me if
they didn't always
see the fight in me.
Muscle memory tightens me.
I really want to like them too.
I never wanted more foes than
friends are vital, and I am
starved of this wonderful.

I am not so hard,
not too strong
and independent.
I want to love
immensely
shine iridescently,
but you must let me.
Take your hand
off my candlelight.
When I glow,
it is better for the room.

It is lonely in this life,
but mine is unfairly.
Must I prove my worth
to all who dare me?

They saw my will to survive,
and thought me to be a killing.
Although Black girls are magic,
we are still human.

I do not want self-preservation.
I want to age gracefully.
Allow me to be gentle;
accept this affirmation.

QUEER ERASURE

I once wrote a poem
about the first woman
I loved.
I even slammed it a few times,
and it scored fine.

It was kind of kinky
and carefully cliché
and no one really
thought it was about me
because I didn't really
talk about those things.
Y'know—liking women,
and that's only the beginning.
(I recently decided I was pan too.)

I guess I was working
hard in the closet, because
I can't find it.
The poem.
How will people know,
I loved her so?

I'VE BEEN SO MAD AT YOU

So mad so mad
But we are just figuring this shit out
We are just doing the best we can for ourselves—
I don't blame you.
For putting yourself first.
I just miss you so bad
I just wish you were here
At the breakfast nook
Battle rapping with me
Telling me I'm dumb
For giving boys a second chance
Telling me I'm ugly
And I'll tell you you're uglier
And we make that shit beautiful
Just like we could
Just like we did
Making shit look better
Than what it really is

WHEN I LOSE MY MOTHER

I will lose
oatmeal baths
Benadryl to sleep
let me smell your breath
stop scratching
smack on hand
go brush your teeth

I will lose
working mom
pencil skirt suit
cursive signatures
honey caramel blonde
my only sunshine

I will lose
you should've known better
whooping or grounding
go read a book
go sit down somewhere

I will lose
maternal bosom
overused night gown
shoulder to cry on

I will lose
somebody's praying for me
holy lesbian temple

I will lose
lovely lamenting lace

I will lose

GLORIA: FOREVER FIRST LADY

Buoyant brown skin
organza on a wide brim
feathers rhinestones
bows and flowers
hair perfectly curled and silver
sitting underneath her church hat

sparkly suit set
maven of Macy's
crystal kitten heels
metallic nails
cocktail ring
red-toned lipstick
and don't forget
statement necklace

And yes,
the purse matches,
so it looks good
when she opens it
and opens it, she does
because she gives
like her life depends on it
even when we do not deserve it.
I imagine she thinks
who is she to judge?
Leave that to the Father.

Don't call her a prayer warrior.
Call her a prayer peacemaker,
how she tranquils you
into an amen.

When my Granny says
I am in her prayers,
I hear "I love you."
I hear "You are healed."
I pray too.

My Granny G is
glorious humility.
Citizen of the city.

Milwaukee's abbey,
a canary of the pulpit;
she sings because she is happy.
You cannot talk about Gloria
without talking about God,
and how good he is.
You cannot talk about
Pastor Joe Allen Sr.
without talking about Gloria.
You cannot talk about
Joe Allen Jr.
without talking about
April 11th, 1964.
Gloria is such a woman
she gave birth to her
second son on the day
she was born.
Joe may have been a gift to her,
but we know Gloria was the reward,
after all. He is the son of the woman
everyone calls mom.

They say a preacher's wife
is an extension of her husband,
but my Granny G is her own person.

She says, "I didn't try to be like him.
I just tried to be a good woman."

Born in 1942.
Bachelor's in business
Master's in religion
President of the
ministers' wives' group.
Ran a computer center
ran a childcare center
ran women's ministry
For eight years,
treasurer of the
international
minister's wives group
but if you ask her,
her pride and joy are her children.

Uncle Kevin born October 15th, 1962.
born with congenital glaucoma
he could see some things
but didn't have complete vision
eventually he was Providence's musician.

My grandmother is
everyone's grandmother,
and I am happy to share her.

I asked her:
What do you want people to remember you by?
She said,
"Well, it really doesn't matter.
I would help people.
I was friend to mankind."

I asked her:
What are you about?
She said,
"I ain't about nothing but getting well."

I talked to my Granny,
who is not yet eighty,
who outlived the men
of our kin. Now, I pray
for her because I know
not the pain that is.

May this poem
immortalize my
grandmother.
May she live
until she's
ready to go.

Let there be
something in me
that is all her.

Let no one
bury her
before she's
gone.

Long Live Granny G,
Forever First Lady.

A WALK IN THE PINES

is not the same walk
you made with your dog at fourteen,
but it still is a product of social distancing,
wondering when it will all be over.

you walk far:
take in the houses, neighbors, and their cars
wondering where did everybody go.
Deondre does not live in the house
he gave you hickies in,
and Keke's grandma doesn't sale cool cups
no one is fist-fighting
and you wonder when did it get so white here
guess the schools weren't too ghetto after all
and some of the kids you saw then
are not kids at all.
it be like that.

like growing older is like disappearing
like the pavement darkening
like trees blocking the view
from the window
like next door strangers
or maybe it is the park renovation
blue herons in the water
kids riding their bike
police patrolling cascade drive
and the field you used to cut across
has houses on it
cascading in a maze
with kids you won't grow up with
because you are already full grown
and parents you won't meet because they are too old

and you will be too old one day
and the home you grew up in
will be almost unrecognizable
and the neighborhood an apparition
of something that died young.

HYDRANGEAS IN BLOOM

Do not forget the soil you grew from.
It is this soil where you one day bloomed
blue in the nights you cried privately
pink at the thought of your first love
purple in your young woke phase
white when you could not go on
orange because you are still alive,
leaves winding up the wall,
you could go all the way.

You thought no flowers grew
at the kind of place you knew.
You never took the time to prune.

Sometimes, you must cut branches
that insist on being dead so you
can grow. Didn't you know?
There's no tree, building, or
wall that can keep you from
ascension. Be it spring, fall,
summer you can survive
winter, coming back every
year, blossoming beautifully
like not dead yet like you're
not done dancing in the wind.

You thought no flowers grew
at the kind of place you knew.
You never took the time to water you.

You are not a wildflower.
You can't grow in any condition.

Take some time to find what feeds you;
give attention to your substance.
Your existence is not
dependent on someone who
didn't tend to the garden
they kept you in.

The soil is not your fault.
The soil did what it could.
The soil has a life too,
and it is a complicated matter.
Forgive the soil that grew you.
You thought no flowers grew
at the kind of place you knew,
but you are a gift to the ground,
petal's phenomenon, a big bouquet,
a perennial person too bud to pluck.

You are moon dance by firelight,
tequila with a little lime,
a big white wedding
kissing big daddy in a red gown
abaracadabra, you are magic
let's dance! tuff stuff in the limelight
invincible wee white, baby you made it
you are flowers in a dreamscape
a field of coloration
an endless summer,
still in bloom:

blue in the nights you cried privately
pink at the thought of your first love
purple in your young woke phase
white when you could not go on
orange because you are still alive.

ABOUT THE AUTHOR

Jasmine Games (she/her) is a Black and queer spoken word poet and theater practitioner from Houston, TX. She holds a BA in English and Performance Studies from Texas A&M University (2018) and an MFA in Drama and Theatre for Youth and Communities from The University of Texas at Austin (2022). Games is an award-winning poet and practitioner, including the 2021 Sexton Prize for Poetry from the Black Spring Press Group and the 2021 Winifred Ward Scholarship for excellence in youth drama/theatre from the American Alliance for Theatre Education. Working in education and social justice in Austin, TX, she utilizes drama, creative writing, and devised performance to address social (in)justices with participants of all ages. Learn more about Jasmine at jasmineigames.com and follow her on social media @jasminegamespoetry.

ACKNOWLEDGMENTS

Thank you to my parents, Pilar Morgan, Carol Morgan, and Joe Games, who instilled in me the practice of looking it up, writing it down, and giving me something to cry about. Thank you to Giana Blazquez-Bultman, who is friend to me without expectation that I perform as someone else. Thank you to my five siblings and twelve niblings. Thank you to my family and lifelong friends: all of those who came before us and all of those who will come after us. I love you because you are. You love me because I am.

Thank you to Brandy Barfield Rood and Ricjuane Jenkins for being invested in my poetic journey from day one. Thank you to Florence Davies and Faith Hillis for supporting, protecting, and inspiring me. Thank you to Dr. Megan Alrutz and Katie Dawson for nurturing my scholarship with a rigorous care to my personhood.

Thank you to the poets that kept me: Shailen Scott and Emmalee Newman. Please never stop writing and amplifying your work. Thank you to the young poets of Courageous Cadence. Thank you to my two mentees, Drea McAlister and Alexandria Alivia Collins. Whatever you do, I will be honored to be alongside you.

Thank you to The Black Spring Press Group: Dr. Todd Swift, Edwin Smet, Amira Ghanim, and Caitlin Robson for your endless supports and efforts. Thank you to Cornelius Eady, who chose my work among other wonderful poets. Thank you to these Austin non-profit organizations that act as my co-conspirators:

The VORTEX, Austin Bat Cave, and The African American Youth Harvest Foundation. Thank you to Mic Check Poetry. Thank you to The Austin Poetry Slam. Thank you to Ebony Stewart for your kind words and for your life's work that affirmed my childhood dreams.

Thank you to the communities I intersect and interact with. Thank you to the communities I have yet to know because I am still figuring out who I am. As I grow older, I learn that my life has so much more importance when my existence is intertwined with someone else's.

Finally, thank you to me for staying alive.

Thank you the earth and the universe that holds us. May we be kinder to you.

Thank you, God. Thank you, God.

"Double Dutch" and earlier versions of "Views from Wash Day" and "Winter Funeral," entitled "Over" and "Dead of Winter," were published in Texas A&M University's Black Box Writer residency, sponsored by The University Writing Center and The Department of English.